A Study Guide on the Best-Selling Book

TRUSTING GOD

JERRY BRIDGES

NAVPRESS

A MINISTRY OF THE NAVIGATORS
P.O. BOX 35001, COLORADO SPRINGS, COLORADO 80935

The Navigators is an international Christian organization. Jesus Christ gave His followers the Great Commission to go and make disciples (Matthew 28:19). The aim of The Navigators is to help fulfill that commission by multiplying laborers for Christ in every nation.

NavPress is the publishing ministry of The Navigators. NavPress publications are tools to help Christians grow. Although publications alone cannot make disciples or change lives, they can help believers learn biblical discipleship, and apply what they learn to their lives and ministries.

ISBN 08910-92412

Sixth printing, 1992

Scripture quotations in this publication are from the *Holy Bible: New International Version* (NIV). Copyright © 1973, 1978, 1984, International Bible Society. Used by permission of Zondervan Bible Publishers.

Printed in the United States of America

CONTENTS

AUTHOR

Jerry Bridges is Vice President for Corporate Affairs of The Navigators. He grew up in Tyler, Texas, and is a graduate of the University of Oklahoma.

While serving as an officer in the United States Navy, Jerry came in contact with The Navigators and soon felt God's call on his life to that ministry. He has served on The Navigators' staff since 1955.

Jerry combines a Bible teaching ministry with his corporate responsibilities for The Navigators. He is also the author of four books: *The Pursuit of Holiness, The Practice of Godliness, Trusting God,* and *Transforming Grace.*

HOW TO USE THIS STUDY GUIDE

Many Christians wish to develop a deeper trust in God. This study is designed to be used with the book *Trusting God* by Jerry Bridges (NavPress, 1988), but it can also be used by itself. The guide will help apply the truths of the book to your personal experience, and give you a chance to interact with relevant Scripture passages. The guide can be used for individual or group study.

Preparing the Lesson
Each lesson has four sections.

1. Central Idea. This section states the main point of the lesson. It will be helpful to keep this in mind while preparing the study, as well as during discussions with a group.

2. Examining Trust. This section is representative of the chapters in *Trusting God*. The study guide can be used alone, but reading the chapters in *Trusting God* is strongly encouraged. Members of a group should read this section before meeting.

3. Developing Trust. These questions should be answered by group members before the group meeting. Some questions are based on Scripture verses; others, on the section "Examining Trust." The better prepared group members are, the better the discussion will be. Ask the Holy Spirit to bring to mind experiences you have had that you can use to better understand the truths taught in certain questions. Past experiences and lessons learned can be shared without revealing confidential details. If you have no personal experience that relates to a particular question, think about a person you know who has had a relevant experience and try to draw on his or her experience.

4. Trust in Action. Make a personal commitment to do at least one thing from this section each week You should read this section early in the week so that you have plenty of time for whatever you decide to do. Be ready to share your experiences with your group.

Leading a Group

Groups vary, and the leader must be sensitive to the needs of his or her group. It is a good idea to dedicate each meeting to the Lord with an opening prayer. The leader can ask for a volunteer to open in prayer or can ask a specific person ahead of time. Having different people open with prayer will give many members this privilege and will lend some variety.

If you have someone who can lead a time of singing, this is a good way to worship together. During this singing time you may want to share Scripture verses that members have been memorizing. The verses can be shared before the singing or between songs in a mood of worship. Members should not feel pressured to memorize Scripture but should have the opportunity to share what they have learned.

Next, move into the material to be covered. If your group has prepared ahead of time, you can go right into the questions. If not, you will want to read the "Examining Trust" section together. Leaders should decide which questions to cover during group time. You probably will not have time to discuss all questions in depth. Focus on the ones that are most important for your group. When a question is about a Scripture passage, it will be helpful to read the passage together. When there are a number of passages, decide which ones to discuss during group time.

Keep your group focused on understanding and applying the truths presented each week. You can minimize controversy by avoiding detailed discussions of conflicting viewpoints. Emphasize what members agree on, and accept differences of opinion without contention.

Close your time together with prayer. The leader is responsible to watch the time and to save enough time for prayer. This time is the "heart" of any group and will bind a group together more than anything else. It is better to cut discussion short than to neglect prayer. To avoid spending all your prayer time taking requests, ask members to bring up requests during prayer, explaining important details as they pray. You can talk later about what you have prayed for. Encourage spontaneous prayer. Ask people to pray for one request at a time and to feel free to pray several times. Vary your group prayer time. For instance, you can introduce subjects of prayer with verses from your study and let people pray as they are led.

1

CAN YOU TRUST GOD?

Central Idea
God is completely sovereign, infinite in wisdom, perfect in love, and therefore worthy of our trust. God's desire for us is that we learn to trust Him.

Examining Trust
Learning to trust God has been a slow and difficult process for me. It is a process that is still under way. But several years ago, in an effort to strengthen my own trust in God, I began a lengthy Bible study on the subject of God's sovereignty in the affairs of His people. That study has helped me immeasurably, and it is the fruit of that study I now share with you. This is written from the perspective of a brother and companion to all those who are tempted at times to ask, "Can I really trust God?"

Adversity is difficult even when we know God is in control of our circumstances. In fact, that knowledge sometimes tends to aggravate the pain. "If God is in control," we ask, "why did He allow this to happen?"

All of us experience adversity at different times and in varying degrees throughout our lives. "Man is born to adversity as surely as sparks fly upward" (Job 5:7). Adversity and its accompanying emotional pain comes in many forms. Some pain is sudden, traumatic, and devastating.

Other adversities are chronic, persistent, and seemingly designed to wear down our spirits over time. Even those whose lives are free from major pain still experience the frequently frustrating or anxiety-producing events of daily life which momentarily grab our attention and rob us of our peace of mind. It is in the crucible of even this minor level of adversity that we are tempted to wonder, "Can I trust God?"

I have spent a good portion of my adult life encouraging people to pursue holiness; to obey God. Yet, I acknowledge it often seems more difficult to trust God than to obey Him. The moral will of God given to us in the Bible is rational and reasonable. The circumstances in which we must trust God often appear irrational and inexplicable. The law of God is readily recognized to be good for us, even when we don't want to obey it. The circumstances of our lives frequently appear to be dreadful and grim or perhaps even calamitous and tragic. Obeying God is worked out within well-defined boundaries of God's revealed will. Trusting God is worked out in an arena that has no boundaries. We are always coping with the unknown.

It is just as important to trust God as it is to obey Him. When we disobey God we defy His authority and despise His holiness. But when we fail to trust God we doubt His sovereignty and question His goodness. In both cases we cast aspersions upon His majesty and His character. God views our distrust of Him as seriously as He views our disobedience.

The Scriptures teach us three essential truths about God—truths we must believe if we are to trust Him in adversity. They are:

- God is completely sovereign.
- God is infinite in wisdom.
- God is perfect in love.

Someone has expressed these three truths as they relate to us in this way: "God in His love always wills what is best for us. In His wisdom He always knows what is

12

best, and in His sovereignty He has the power to bring it about."

The sovereignty of God is asserted, either expressly or implicitly, on almost every page of the Bible. Rather than being offended over the Bible's assertion of God's sovereignty in both good and calamity, believers should be comforted by it. Whatever our particular calamity or adversity may be, we may be sure that our Father has a loving purpose in it. As King Hezekiah said, "Surely it was for my benefit that I suffered such anguish" (Isaiah 38:17). God does not exercise His sovereignty capriciously, but only in such a way as His infinite love deems best for us.

God's sovereignty is also exercised in infinite wisdom, far beyond our ability to comprehend. God's plan and His ways of working out His plan are frequently beyond our ability to fathom and understand. We must learn to trust when we don't understand. *(Taken from the preface and chapter 1 of* Trusting God.)

Developing Trust

1. Do you have a harder time trusting God in the major trials of your life or in relatively minor things? Explain why you think this is the case.

2. Do you think Christians struggle more with questions and uncertainties in the midst of adversity than nonbelievers? Why or why not?

3. a. According to Proverbs 27:1, what should be our perspective on the future?

b. How does this affect our need to trust God?

4. God desires that we learn to trust Him. What do you learn about trust from these verses?

Psalm 32:10

Proverbs 3:5

John 14:1

5. a. What is the difference between trusting God and obeying Him?

b. How are trusting God and obedience related?

c. Is it easier for you to trust God or to be obedient? Explain why.

d. Describe a situation in your life where obedience and trusting were both important.

e. Describe a time when trusting God made it easier to be obedient.

6. Read Psalm 78:9-22.

a. What attitude did the Israelites reveal in the desert?

b. What was God's reaction to their attitude?

c. Describe a time when your attitude was similar to that of the Israelites.

d. How do you think God felt about your attitude? (See Hebrews 11:6 and Philippians 2:14.)

e. What in your life indicated how God felt?

7. According to Isaiah 55:9 and Romans 11:33, why is it important for us to trust God even when we don't understand what He is doing?

8. a. What do these verses say about our privilege of knowing God?

Psalm 9:10

Jeremiah 9:23-24

Philippians 3:8-11

b. Knowing God is more than simply knowing facts about Him. What does it mean to know God?

c. What are you doing to get to know God better?

d. Do you need to make or renew your commitments to these actions?

e. Write a prayer in which you express your desire to know God more intimately.

Trust in Action
Choose one or more of these ideas to work on. Groups may want to allow time each week to share experiences from this section.

1. Keep a journal while studying this book. Record all the circumstances in which you see God's control and guidance in your life. Beginning this log now will help you see concrete evidence for truths discussed in later chapters.

2. Memorize Psalm 32:10.

3. Make a commitment to memorize Romans 8:18-39. This may seem like an overwhelming task, but if the passage is broken down into small sections, it can be memorized fairly easily. The rewards of having this amazing passage memorized will be more than worth the effort.

4. Think of a relationship in which you have trusted another person. Write a letter to this person and share your thoughts from this lesson. Tell this person how much you value his or her trustworthiness.

5. Ask God for the opportunity to share something about His trustworthiness with an unbeliever. Watch for the opportunity and take advantage of it.

2

IS GOD IN CONTROL?

Central Idea
God is in control. He has a purpose and a plan for you, and He has the power to carry out that plan.

Examining Trust
God is sovereign (all-powerful) and He is good. God's providence is a term we often use in Christian parlance to acknowledge God's seeming intervention in our affairs. There are two things wrong, however, with the way in which we refer to the providence of God. For one, we almost always use the expression "the providence of God" in connection with apparently "good" events. God controls both the good and the bad. God has not looked the other way or been caught by surprise when adversity strikes us. He is in control of the adversity, directing it to His glory and our good.

The second problem with our popular use of the expression "the providence of God" is that we either unconsciously or deliberately imply that God intervenes at specific points in our lives but is largely only an interested spectator most of the time.

God's providence is His constant care for and His absolute rule over all His creation for His own glory and the good of His people. Note the twofold objective of

God's providence: His glory and the good of His people. These two objectives are never antithetical; they are always in harmony with each other.

The Bible teaches that God not only created the universe, but that He upholds and sustains it day by day, hour by hour. Scripture says, "The Son is . . . sustaining all things by His powerful word" (Hebrews 1:3), and "in him all things hold together" (Colossians 1:17).

The Bible also teaches that God governs the universe, not only inanimate creation, but also the actions of all creatures, both men and animals. He is called the Ruler of all things (1 Chronicles 29:12), the blessed and only Ruler (1 Timothy 6:15).

Randomness, luck, chance, fate. This is modern man's answer to the age-old question, "Why?" Even many Christians who accept the concept of God's sovereignty believe that He chooses not to exercise His sovereignty in the daily affairs of our lives. Christians are often unwilling to accept the fact that God is working, because they don't understand *how* He is working. They have chosen to substitute the doctrine of chance for the doctrine of divine providence.

I admit that we are often unable to reconcile God's sovereignty and goodness in the face of widespread tragedy or personal adversity, but I believe that, although we often do not understand God's ways, He is sovereignly at work in all of our circumstances.

If there is a single event in all of the universe that can occur outside of God's sovereign control then we cannot trust Him. His love may be infinite, but if His power is limited and His purpose can be thwarted, we cannot trust Him. He permits, for reasons known only to Himself, people to act contrary to and in defiance of His revealed will. But He never permits them to act contrary to His sovereign will.

One of our problems with the sovereignty of God is that it frequently does not appear that God is in control of the circumstances of our lives. It is difficult to see God working through secondary causes and frail, sinful human beings. But it is the ability of God to so arrange diverse human actions to fulfill His purpose that makes His sovereignty marvelous and yet mysterious.

No one can act and no circumstances can occur outside the bounds of God's sovereign will. But this is only one side of His sovereignty. The other side, which is just ~God's~ as important to our trusting Him, is that no plan of God's ~plan~ can be thwarted. God has an over-arching purpose for all ~for us.~ believers: to conform us to the likeness of His Son, Jesus Christ (Romans 8:29). He also has a specific purpose for each of us that is His unique, tailor-made plan for our individual life (see Ephesians 2:10).

I readily admit it is difficult to believe God is in control when we are in the midst of anxiety, heartache, or grief. We must learn to obey God one choice at a time; we ~1 circumstance~ must also learn to trust God one circumstance at a time. ~at a time~ Trusting God is not a matter of my feelings but of my will. That act of the will must be based on belief, and belief must be based on truth.

We must believe the truth that God carries out His own good purposes without ever being thwarted, and He so directs and controls all events and all actions of His creatures that they never act outside of His sovereign will. That which should distinguish the suffering of believers from unbelievers is the confidence that our suffering is under the control of an all-powerful and all-loving God; our suffering has meaning and purpose in God's eternal plan, and He brings or allows to come into our lives only that which is for His glory and our good. *(Taken from chapters 2 and 3 of* Trusting God.*)*

Developing Trust

1. a. What is God's providence? (The "Examining Trust" section may help you answer these questions.)

b. What is the purpose or objective of God's providence?

c. Describe a situation in your life when God's will and your best interests seemed to be in conflict.

d. How was this conflict resolved?

2. What do the following verses say about God's providence?

Psalm 31:15 "My times are in your hands"

Psalm 147:8-9 Looks after & provides

Acts 17:24-28 Everything we do is because of God

2 Corinthians 9:10 God supplies everything for us.

3. What specific evidence of God's sustaining presence in the universe is most dramatic to you? (Illustrations from science would be appropriate here.)

4. a. In what ways do people see God's providence as limited?

b. Do you think of God's providence as limited? Explain.

c. In what ways do you act as though God's providence is limited even though you may believe that it isn't?

5. a. Restate Matthew 10:29-31 in your own words.

b. Think about a person who sees chance or randomness as the explanation for all that happens. How would this philosophy affect his or her life?

c. What would such a person value?

d. How does Matthew 10:29-31 refute such a perspective?

6. a. Do you believe that God is active in the daily affairs of your life?

b. What evidence do you see, from your past or present, for His involvement in your life? (If you have begun keeping a journal, it may help you answer this question.)

7. There is an invisible war being waged between God and Satan, and our lives are often the battleground. What do the following passages say about Satan's ability to touch us?

Job 1:12, 2:6

God is in control of how much we are tempted.

Luke 22:31-32

8. God never permits people to act contrary to His sovereign will. How do the following verses support this statement?

Proverbs 16:9   *Lord determines his steps*

Proverbs 19:21   *The Lords purpose prevails*

Lamentations 3:37   *The Lord must decree what man wants to happen.*

James 4:13-15   *Say "If the Lord wills"*

(For additional study see Proverbs 21:30, Ecclesiastes 7:13, and Revelation 3:7.)

9. What conclusions about God and what He does can you draw from these verses?

Job 42:2   *No plan can be Thwarted*

Psalm 115:3   *God does what he pleases*

Isaiah 46:10 *My purpose will stand*

Daniel 4:34-35

(For additional verses see Isaiah 14:27, 43:13; and Ephesians 1:11-12.)

10. In his book *When Bad Things Happen to Good People*, Rabbi Harold Kushner concludes that God cannot be both sovereign and good, and so Kushner chooses to believe in a God who is good.

　　a. What do you think about Rabbi Kushner's conclusion?

　　b. How do you reconcile God's goodness and His sovereignty? That is, if God is able to prevent evil, and if He is committed to good, then why doesn't He prevent evil?

11. We need to be very sensitive in teaching others about the sovereignty of God and encouraging them to trust God when they are in the midst of problems or pain. It is much easier to trust in the sovereignty of God when it is the other person who is hurting. We need to be like Jesus, of whom it was said, "A bruised reed he will not break" (Matthew 12:20). Job lost his children, his wealth, and his health. His friends preached to him about God's sovereignty. Read Job's response to his friends in Job 6:14-27.

a. What did Job's friends do wrong? How did they "bruise" him?

b. If you had a friend in Job's position, how would you deal with him when he questioned God's sovereignty and goodness?

Trust in Action

1. Choose one of the following Bible characters and read his or her story. Briefly summarize how God guided the events in this person's life. Remember that these stories were given to us for encouragement (Romans 15:4). What God did for these people He will do for you.

Ruth: Ruth 1–4
Esther: Esther 1–10
Joseph: Genesis 37, 39–45

2. Think of someone you know who is in a difficult situation. Express God's love to him or her in a tangible way (prepare a meal, write a note of encouragement, offer to help with household repairs, etc.).

3. Memorize Romans 8:28-29.

3

GOD'S SOVEREIGNTY OVER PEOPLE

Central Idea
God works in the hearts of people to move them to fulfill His purposes. Any treatment, good or bad, that we receive from another can be seen as part of God's plan for us.

Examining Trust
We are, from a human point of view, often at the mercy of other people and their decisions or actions. Sometimes those decisions or actions are benevolent and good; sometimes they are wicked or careless. Either way they do affect us, often in a significant way. How are we to respond when we find ourselves seemingly in the hands of someone else, when we desperately need a favorable decision or a favorable action on that person's part? Can we trust God that He can and will work in the heart of that individual to bring about His plan for us?

Or consider the instance when someone is out to harm us, to ruin our reputation, or to jeopardize our career: Can we trust God to intervene in the heart of that person so that he does not carry out his evil intent? According to the Bible, the answer in both instances is yes.

Perhaps the clearest biblical statement that God does sovereignly influence the decisions of people is found in

Proverbs 21:1: "The king's heart is in the hand of the LORD; he directs it like a watercourse wherever he pleases." The stubborn will of the most powerful monarch on earth is directed by God as easily as the farmer directs the flow of water in his irrigation canals. The argument, then, is from the greater to the lesser—if God controls the king's heart, surely He controls everyone else's.

God can and does move in the hearts of people to show favor to us when that favor will accomplish His purpose. Furthermore, when necessary, God restrains people from decisions or actions that would harm us. Of course, God does not always restrain the wicked and harmful actions of others toward His people. We do not know why God sometimes allows our enemies to prevail and sometimes restrains them. It is enough to know that God can and does restrain the harmful acts of others toward us when that is His sovereign will.

You can trust God in all the areas of your life where you are dependent upon the favor or frown of another person. God will move in that person's heart to carry out His will for you.

The Bible asserts both God's sovereignty and people's freedom and moral responsibility, but it never attempts to explain their relationship. For one thing, God is infinite in His ways as well as His being. A finite mind simply cannot comprehend an infinite being beyond what He has expressly revealed to us. Because of this, some things about God will forever remain a mystery to us. The relationship of the sovereign will of God to the freedom and moral responsibility of people is one of those mysteries.

We must also keep in mind that God is never the author of sin. Though people's sinful intents and actions serve the sovereign purpose of God, we must never conclude that God has induced anyone to sin. God judges people for the very sins that He uses to carry out His purpose.

The Bible consistently portrays people as making real choices of their own will. The choices people make are moral choices; that is people are held accountable by God for the choices they make. God works without violating or coercing people's will; rather He works in His mysterious way through their wills to accomplish His purposes.

There are some cautions we need to consider, lest we wrongly use the doctrine of God's sovereignty over people.

First, we should never use the doctrine as an excuse for our own shortcomings.

Second, we should not allow the doctrine of God's sovereignty to cause us to respond passively to the actions of other people that affect us. The doctrine of God's sovereignty should never be used to promote passivity.

Third, we must never use the doctrine of God's sovereignty to excuse our own sinful actions or decisions that hurt another person. *(Taken from chapter 4 of* Trusting God.*)*

Developing Trust

1. Examine the following Scriptures for evidence of God's work in the hearts of believers and unbelievers. Record the key words used to describe His working.

Ezra 1:1,5; 6:22

Proverbs 21:1

Daniel 1:9

2 Corinthians 8:16-17

Deuteronomy 2:30

Joshua 11:20

2. Read Exodus 4:21 and 8:15.

    a. Who is given the responsibility for Pharaoh's hard heart in each of these verses?

    b. How do these verses, taken side by side, help us see the relationship between man's responsibility and God's work in our hearts?

3. God's restraining influence on people's actions and decisions is seen in the following verses. Complete the chart.

What action did God prevent?	What emotion did God influence?
Genesis 20:1-7	
Genesis 35:5	
Exodus 34:23-24	

4. According to the following verses, how do the sinful actions of man affect God's purposes?

Genesis 50:20

Acts 4:27-28

Revelation 17:15-18

5. Do you agree that a finite mind cannot comprehend an infinite Being beyond what He has expressly revealed? Why or why not?

6. a. God can and does work in the minds and hearts of people to accomplish His will. How should that truth affect your attitude?

b. How should that truth affect the way you pray about your job or other concerns?

7. Why should confidence in God's sovereignty in the lives of people keep us from becoming resentful and bitter when we are treated unjustly or maliciously by others?

8. a. Describe a time when you were treated unfairly.

b. How did you react?

c. To what extent did your reaction show trust in God?

d. Would you like your response to be different next time? If so, how?

e. What was the end result of the situation?

f. What good, if any, came from this situation?

9. What are some specific things you can pray for in your own life this week, knowing that God can work in people's hearts?

10. a. Describe a time recently when you were affected by someone else's decision or action.

   b. At the time how did you feel about the situation?

   c. How do you feel now about the outcome of the situation?

   d. Does your study of God's sovereignty in the hearts of people affect your perspective on what happened? How?

Trust in Action

1. Memorize Deuteronomy 29:29 or Proverbs 21:1.

2. Think of three people you know who need to turn to the Lord. Ask the Lord to work in their hearts.

3. Are there people who have treated you unfairly whom you have not forgiven? Spend some time with the Lord, asking Him to cleanse you of all bitterness toward others. Pray Psalm 51:10.

4

GOD'S RULE OVER
THE NATIONS

Central Idea
God is in control of all nations, shaping events and
decisions to fulfill His purposes.

Examining Trust
As we trace the sovereignty of God through the Bible, one
of the most frequent references to it concerns His sovereignty over nations and governments. God is Lord over all
of human history, and He is working out all the details of
that history, as Paul said in Ephesians 1:11, "in conformity   *Eph 1:11*
with the purpose of his will." That is, God makes all
events of history; all the decisions of rulers, kings, and par-
liaments; and all the actions of their governments, armies,
and navies serve His will.

The fact that God is sovereign over our rulers is usually not evident to us as we view their decisions and actions
on a human plane. For the most part, governmental officials and legislative bodies do their work quite apart from
any intent to carry out the will of God. We see this amply
demonstrated in the life and death of Jesus Christ.

Caesar Augustus issued a decree that a census should
be taken. This required Joseph and Mary to go to the town
of Bethlehem to register at just the right time for the Mes-
siah to be born in Bethlehem in fulfillment of Micah's

prophecy (Micah 5:2). Caesar certainly did not intend to be an instrument to fulfill any Jewish prophecy, yet that is exactly what he was.

We should likewise see in those affairs reported in our daily paper the sovereign hand of God just as much as we see it in the Bible. Of course, we don't have the advantage of the divinely revealed explanation of today's events, as we do of those recorded in the Bible, but that does not make God's sovereign rule today any less certain. God recorded in His Word specific instances of His sovereign rule over history in order that we might trust Him in the affairs of history as they unfold before us today.

The Scriptures teach the following specific truths about the sovereignty of God over the nations:

1. God in His sovereignty has established government for the good of all people—believers as well as unbelievers (Romans 13:1-4).

2. God determines who rules in those governments (Daniel 4:17).

3. God determines the timing of each leader's rule (Isaiah 40:23-24).

4. God controls the decisions that rulers make (Proverbs 16:33).

5. God rules in the victories and defeats between nations on the battlefield (Proverbs 21:31).

God sometimes causes government leaders or officials to make foolish decisions in order to bring judgment upon a nation. We should take more seriously our responsibility to pray for the leaders of our government that they will make wise decisions. Although we may suspect that some of the more disastrous decisions are evidence of God's judgment, we do not know that. We do know God has instructed us to pray for leaders. Our duty, then, is to pray for wise decisions, but to trust God when foolish and harmful decisions are made.

As we look around the world today what do we see? We see over one-half of the world's population living in countries whose governments are hostile to the gospel, where missionaries are not allowed, and where national Christians are severely hindered from proclaiming Christ. As we look at these conditions we must also look at the sovereignty of God and at His promises. He has promised to redeem people from every nation, and He has commanded us to make disciples of all nations. We must, then, trust God by praying. Some will go to those nations as God opens doors, but all of us must pray. We must learn to trust God, not only in the adverse circumstances of our individual lives, but also in the adverse circumstances of the Church as a whole.

God is sovereign over the nations. He is sovereign over the officials of our own government in all their actions as they affect us directly. He is sovereign over the officials of government in lands where our brothers and sisters in Christ suffer for their faith in Him. And He is sovereign over the nations where every attempt is made to stamp out true Christianity. In all of these areas, we can and must trust God. *(Taken from chapter 5 of* Trusting God.*)*

Developing Trust

1. There are many events that took place during the life of Jesus that show how government officials, acting freely, fulfilled the purposes of God. Fill in the following chart.

Name of ruler	Official action	Prophecy fulfilled
Matthew 2:13-16 Herod	tried to kill Jesus	Hosea 11:1 out of Egypt I called My Son
Matthew 2:17-18 Herod	killed children in Bethlehem	Jeremiah 31:15 Death of children
Matthew 2:21-23 Archelaus	moved to Nazareth	Isaiah 9:1 Moved to the North

Name of ruler	Official action	Prophecy fulfilled
Luke 2:1-4 *Tax Caesar*	*Ceasar issued a Tax*	Micah 5:2 *Messiah to be born in Bethlehem*
Acts 4:27-28 *Herod Pilot*	*Conspired against Christ*	Isaiah 53:3-6 *Rejected by men*

2. What truths are taught about governments and rulers in the following verses?

Proverbs 16:9,33 *The Lord determines actions*

Proverbs 21:31 *Victory is in the Lord hands*

Isaiah 40:22-24 *Sets up & tears down rulers.*

Daniel 4:17 *God determines rulers*

Daniel 4:31-32 *God takes away rulers authority*

Romans 13:1-4 *God establishes authority & we are to serve our rulers*

3. What responsibilities do we have toward our government?

Romans 13:1-7 *obey Pay taxes respect honor.*

40

1 Timothy 2:1-4

Requests, prayers & thanksgiving

4. a. Describe a time in your life when a governmental decision had an effect on your life (for example, military draft, new tax laws, zoning regulation, etc.).

b. To what extent did you see God's hand in the events at the time?

c. From your present perspective, what do you think God was doing in that situation?

5. a. Read 2 Samuel 15:1-16 and 16:20–17:14. Why did God want Absalom to follow the poor advice of Hushai?

b. What might be God's purpose in allowing rulers to make foolish decisions?

c. Does God protect His people from the consequences of these poor decisions? Why or why not?

6. According to Daniel 9:1-19, what was Daniel's response when he realized that Israel's exile in Babylon was almost over?

7. a. What is promised in the following verses?

Matthew 28:18-20

Christ gives us all authority and is with us to the end of the age

Revelation 7:9-10

God wants to save people out of every nation.

b. How can you respond to these promises?

8. a. What are your general thoughts about the present world situation?

b. Did the truths in this chapter change your perspective on current events? If so, how?

Trust in Action

1. Spend some time with the Lord doing some soul searching about your role in the political process of your country. Is God prompting you to a deeper involvement?

2. Write to your government representatives letting them know what you think about some issue currently being debated.

3. Choose several world leaders and make a commitment to pray regularly for them. Make an effort to read articles about these leaders and their lives.

4. Choose one group of missionaries and pray regularly for them. Or choose one nation that is currently hostile to the gospel and pray regularly that God will open doors in that country.

5. Memorize Psalm 33:16-17.

5

GOD'S POWER OVER NATURE

Central Idea
God has established certain physical laws for the
operation of His universe. Moment by moment those
laws operate according to His direct will.

Examining Trust
God has not walked away from the day-to-day control of
His creation. Certainly He has established physical laws by
which He governs the forces of nature, but those laws con-
tinuously operate according to His sovereign will. The
Bible teaches that God controls all the forces of nature,
both destructive and productive, on a continuous,
moment-by-moment basis. All expressions of nature, all
occurrences of weather, whether it be a devastating tornado or a gentle rain on a spring day, are acts of God.

Many sensitive Christians struggle over the multitude
of large-scale natural disasters around the world—an
earthquake in one place, famine in another, typhoons and
floods somewhere else. Thousands of people are killed,
others starve to death. "Why does God allow all this?" we
may ask.

It is not wrong to wrestle with these issues, as long as
we do it in a reverent and submissive attitude toward God.
Indeed, to fail to wrestle with the issue of large-scale

tragedy may indicate a lack of compassion toward others on our part. However, we must be careful not to, in our minds, take God off His throne of absolute sovereignty or put Him in the dock and bring Him to the bar of our judgment.

God brings Himself into these events. He said in Isaiah 45:7, "I form the light and create darkness, I bring prosperity and create disaster; I, the LORD, do all these things." God Himself accepts the responsibility, so to speak, of disasters. He actually does more than accept the responsibility; He actually claims it. In effect, God says, "I, and I alone, have the power and authority to bring about both prosperity and disaster, both weal and woe, both good and bad."

We obviously do not understand why God creates disaster, or why He brings it to one town and not to another. We recognize, too, that just as God sends His sun and rain on both the righteous and the unrighteous, so He also sends the tornado, or the hurricane, or the earthquake on both. God's sovereignty over nature does not mean that Christians never encounter the tragedies of natural disaster.

Illness and physical affliction is another area in which we struggle to trust God. When God called Moses to lead the Israelites out of Egypt, Moses protested his inadequacy, including the fact that he was slow of speech. God's reply to Moses is very instructive to us in this area of physical affliction, for God said, "Who gave man his mouth? Who makes him deaf or mute? Who gives him sight or makes him blind? Is it not I, the LORD?" (Exodus 4:11). Here God specifically ascribes to His own work the physical afflictions of deafness, muteness, and blindness.

Afflictions don't "just happen." They are all within the sovereign will of God. Such a statement immediately brings us into the problem of pain and suffering. Why does a sovereign God who loves us allow such pain and heartache?

Briefly, we know that all creation has been subjected to frustration because of the sin of Adam (Romans 8:20). So we can say that the ultimate cause of all pain and suffering must be traced back to the Fall. God's weal and woe are not arbitrary or capricious, but His determined response to man's sin. The sovereign God who subjected creation to frustration still rules over it, pain and all.

God never wastes pain. He always uses it to accomplish His purpose. And His purpose is for His glory and our good. Therefore, we can trust Him when our hearts are aching or our bodies are racked with pain. *(Taken from chapter 6 of* Trusting God.*)*

Developing Trust

1. Summarize in your own words what each of these verses says about God's role in natural phenomena.

Job 37:3,6,10-13

Psalm 147:8,16-18

Jeremiah 10:13, 14:22

Amos 4:7-9

2. a. What is your usual attitude toward the weather? Do you tend to complain about it? thank God for it? feel that God isn't responsible?

b. Is your attitude generally pleasing to God? Why or why not?

3. a. What is God taking responsibility for in Exodus 4:11 and Isaiah 45:7?

b. What are some possible responses to these passages?

c. Which response do you choose? Why?

4. Read John 9:1-3. Explain in your own words the reason Jesus gives for the man's blindness.

5. a. What does God teach us about the conception of children in these verses?

Genesis 16:2

Genesis 29:31

Judges 13:3

1 Samuel 1:5

Psalm 139:13

b. If a couple is unable to have children, how can these verses help them maintain a trusting attitude toward God?

6. The idea that God claims responsibility for deadly earthquakes, droughts, blindness, and childlessness prompts sensitive people to ask questions. Certainly we can't learn much without asking questions.

a. Are there limits to the kinds of questions we should ask of God? If so, what limits? If not, why not?

b. Can we expect God to answer our questions? Why or why not?

c. What kinds of attitudes are acceptable when questioning God?

d. What kinds of attitudes are unacceptable?

e. Give some possible reasons why God leaves many of our questions unanswered.

7. a. Describe an experience in your life that caused you to doubt God's control and to ask why.

b. What answers did you get to your questioning?

c. Did anything good come from that experience? If so, what was it?

8. How can coming to grips with the fact that God is in control of nature affect your daily life, especially your current circumstances?

Trust in Action
1. Read the book of Job in one sitting. What was God's answer to all Job's questionings?

2. Memorize Habakkuk 3:17-19.

3. Get involved in some form of crisis intervention in your community (for example, emergency relief, pregnancy counseling, helping battered women or abused children, etc.).

6

GOD'S SOVEREIGNTY AND OUR RESPONSIBILITY

Central Idea
We are responsible for all our actions. We must seek God in prayer, act with prudence at all times, and trust God to work out His good purposes in our lives.

Examining Trust
There is no conflict between trusting God and accepting our responsibility. Our duty is found in the revealed will of God in the Scriptures. Our trust must be in the sovereign will of God, as He works in the ordinary circumstances of our daily lives for our good and His glory.

Knowledge of His sovereignty is meant to be an encouragement to pray, not an excuse to lapse into a sort of pious fatalism. Prayer assumes the sovereignty of God. If God is not sovereign, we have no assurance that He is able to answer our prayers. God's sovereignty, along with His wisdom and love, is the foundation of our trust in Him; prayer is the expression of that trust. God's sovereignty does not negate our responsibility to pray, but rather makes it possible to pray with confidence.

God's sovereignty also does not negate our responsibility to act prudently. To act prudently means to use all legitimate, biblical means at our disposal to avoid harm to ourselves or others and to bring about what we believe to be the right course of events.

One of the most basic means of prudence that God has given to us is prayer. We must not only pray for His overruling providence in our lives, but we must also pray for wisdom to rightly understand our circumstances and use the means He has given us. Another means of prudence God has given us is the opportunity to seek wise and godly counsel.

Prayer is the acknowledgment of God's sovereignty and of our dependence upon Him to act on our behalf. Prudence is the acknowledgment of our responsibility to use all legitimate means.

All of our plans, all of our efforts, and all of our prudence is of no avail unless God prospers those means. Psalm 127:1 says, "Unless the LORD builds the house, its builders labor in vain. Unless the LORD watches over the city, the watchmen stand guard in vain." In this passage there is the concept of both offensive and defensive efforts—of both building for progress and watching against destruction. In a sense, the verse sums up all of our responsibilities in life. Whether it be in the physical, the mental, or the spiritual, we should always be building and watching. And Psalm 127:1 says none of those efforts will prosper unless God intervenes in them.

The psalmist does not say, "Unless God blesses or helps the builders and the watchmen, their efforts are in vain." Rather, he speaks in terms of God Himself building the house and watching over the city. At the same time, there is, of course, no suggestion in the text that God replaces the builders and the watchmen. The obvious meaning is that in every respect we are dependent upon God to enable us and prosper our efforts.

In His infinite wisdom, God's sovereign plan includes our failures and even our sins. God usually works through ordinary events (as opposed to miracles) and the voluntary actions of people. But He always provides the means necessary and guides them by His unseen hand. He is sovereign, and He cannot be frustrated by our failure to act or by our actions, which in themselves are sinful. We must always remember, however, that God still holds us accountable for the very sins that He uses to accomplish His purpose.

There is no conflict in the Bible between His sovereignty and our responsibility. Both concepts are taught with equal force and with never an attempt to "reconcile" them. Let us hold equally to both, doing our duty as it is revealed to us in the Scriptures and trusting God to sovereignly work out His purpose in us and through us. *(Taken from chapter 7 of* Trusting God.*)*

Developing Trust

1. a. Read Nehemiah 4:6-9. In what two ways did the Israelites respond to the threat of attack?

b. What does their response indicate about their understanding of the relationship between prayer and prudence?

2. Meditate on Philippians 4:6-7.

a. Describe a time when you experienced a great deal of anxiety.

b. When you are anxious, do you pray more or less than usual?

c. Is this the way it should be? Explain.

3. a. When we are trusting God and have a peace that comes from Him alone, our prayers are different from when our prayers flow out of anxiety. How are they different?

b. Which way do you pray most often?

c. Choose a difficult situation for which you are presently praying. Write a prayer for that situation from a mind-set of trust.

4. a. Since God is in control and His purpose will inevitably prevail, why do we need to pray?

b. Why do we need to make every effort to act with wisdom?

5. Read Acts 4:23-31.

a. What effect do you think this prayer had on the believers who were praying?

b. What specific requests did the believers make?

c. How does Matthew 28:19-20 help explain their confidence in prayer?

d. What specific applications to your own prayer life can you make from the example of this prayer?

6. Read the account of a violent storm, recorded in Acts 27:13-44.

a. When God revealed that He would deliver Paul and all his shipmates, Paul trusted God and His promise of deliverance. Even so, Paul didn't passively expect God to do the work that He had equipped the sailors to do. Make a list of all the actions that were taken that helped fulfill God's promise that they would all reach land safely.

b. What relationship does this story show between God's sovereignty and our responsibility?

7. Read Psalm 127:1.

a. Are you currently involved in building anything? (This need not be a physical building; it could be an organization, a relationship, etc.) If so, what is it?

b. How is the Lord involved in your building?

c. In what area(s) of your life are you like a watchman guarding a city?

d. How is the Lord involved in your watching?

e. How do you think you should feel and respond, knowing God's involvement in these situations?

8. a. Describe a time when you felt very dependent on God.

b. What did you do for yourself at the time?

c. Did any of your efforts make you less dependent on God? Why or why not?

Trust in Action

1. Read through the book of Proverbs in a modern translation, looking for lessons on prudence. Copy into your journal those verses that especially speak to you.

2. Memorize Philippians 4:6-7.

3. Start a prayer notebook with your requests and God's answers. This can be done very simply, with just a few words for each request. From time to time you may want to write out whole prayers to the Lord. The process of writing prayers causes us to think more seriously about what we are saying to God.

4. Before you go to bed tonight, tell God that you entrust each of your current concerns to Him. Name them. Ask Him to give you wisdom in dealing with each one. Then read Psalm 127:1-2, and go to sleep.

7
THE WISDOM OF GOD

Central Idea
God is infinite in wisdom. He always knows what is best for us, and He knows the best way to bring it about.

Examining Trust

Wisdom is commonly defined as good judgment, or the ability to develop the best course of action, or the best response to a given situation. God's wisdom is intuitive, infinite, and infallible: "His understanding has no limit" (Psalm 147:5).

Nineteenth-century theologian J.L. Dagg said, "God is infinitely wise, because he selects the best possible end of action . . . [and] because he adopts the best possible means for the accomplishment of the end which he has in view."[1] All that God does or allows in all of His creation will ultimately serve His glory.

God's infinite wisdom is displayed in bringing good out of evil, beauty out of ashes. It is displayed in turning all the forces of evil that rage against His children into good for them. But the good that He brings about is often different from the good we envision.

The good that God works for in our lives is conformity to the likeness of His Son. It is not necessarily comfort or happiness but conformity to Christ in ever-increasing measure in this life and in its fullness in eternity. If you stop and think about it, you will realize that most godly character traits can only be developed through adversity.

God in His infinite wisdom knows exactly what adversity we need to grow more and more into the likeness of His Son. He not only knows what we need but when we need it and how best to bring it to pass in our lives.

God never explains to us what He is doing, or why. There is no indication that God ever explained to Job the reasons for all of his terrible sufferings. As readers, we are taken behind the scenes to observe the spiritual warfare between God and Satan, but as far as we can tell from Scripture, God never told Job about that.

We should never ask "why" in the sense of demanding that God explain or justify His actions or what He permits in our lives. I am not talking about the reactive and spontaneous cry of anguish when calamity first befalls us or one we love. Rather, I am speaking of the persistent and demanding "why" that has an accusatory tone toward God in it. The former is a natural human reaction; the latter is a sinful human reaction.

Sometimes we come to the place where we do not demand of God that He explain Himself, but we try to determine or comprehend for ourselves what God is doing. We are unwilling to live without rational reasons for what is happening to us or those we love. We are almost insatiable in our quest for the "why" of the adversity that has come upon us. But this is a futile as well as an untrusting task. God's ways, being the ways of infinite wisdom, simply cannot be comprehended by our finite minds. If we are to find peace for ourselves, we must come to the place where we can honestly say, "God, I do not have to understand. I will just trust You."

It is not only an irreverent act to question God's wisdom; it is also spiritually debilitating. We not only besmirch God's glory; we also deprive ourselves of the comfort and peace that comes by simply trusting Him without requiring an explanation. An unreserved trust of God, when we don't understand what is happening or why, is the only road to peace and comfort and joy. God wants us to honor Him by trusting Him, but He also desires that we experience the peace and joy that come as a result. *(Taken from chapter 8 of* Trusting God.*)*

Developing Trust

✗ **1.** How do these verses describe God's wisdom?

Psalm 147:5 *Without Limit*

Jeremiah 10:12 *God used His wisdom in creation*

Romans 11:33-34 *Gods wisdom is greater then mans ability to understand it.*

2. Are there any past or present events in your life that tempt you to doubt God's wisdom? If so, what are they?

✗ **3.** a. What is the ultimate purpose of all things according to Romans 11:36 and 1 Corinthians 10:31?

   To glorify God.

   b. What does it mean to glorify God?

c. In what ways do you think your present circumstances bring glory to God?

4. Our prayers often seem to go unanswered, yet God is still handling us with wisdom. He knows that the very adversity we long to have removed is His means to help us grow. Read Psalm 119:71.

a. Describe a time when adversity was not removed even though you or others prayed that it would be.

b. Did you experience any personal growth through that adversity? If so, what?

5. What is the logical connection between Romans 8:28 and 8:29? (Notice the word *for* at the beginning of 8:29.)

6. a. Do you think we can fully understand God's reason for any particular event? Why or why not?

b. What attitude is expressed in Job 42:1-3 and Psalm 131:1?

c. What happens when we let go of our questions and trust God?

d. Is it hard for you to let go of your unanswered questions? Why or why not?

7. We should focus not on the reasons for our difficulties but on the lessons we can learn from them.

a. Read Deuteronomy 8:2-5. What lesson did the Israelites learn from their experience of getting only one day's food at a time?

b. Why do you think this lesson would be important for them later when they were prosperous in Canaan? (Read Deuteronomy 8:10-18.)

8. As we read in 2 Samuel 24:10-14, David was more afraid of suffering adversity at the hands of men than from God directly.

a. Why do you think David felt this way?

b. When we are facing adversity from other people, what comfort do Proverbs 21:30 and Romans 8:31 offer us?

9. a. What would you say to a friend who is struggling with the question *why* in the face of difficult circumstances?

b. What kinds of things would you be careful not to say?

Trust in Action

1. Memorize Romans 11:33.

2. Share with a friend something God has been teaching you through this study.

3. Next time you hear of a disaster or tragedy, take time to pray for the people involved.

4. Tell God about the situations in your life, past or present, that tempt you to doubt that He knows what He is doing. Ask Him to help you fully believe that His reasons are good, even though He hasn't shown you what they are. Tell Him exactly how you feel about this situation; then meditate on Psalm 131.

NOTE

1. J.L. Dagg, *Manual of Theology* (Harrisonburg, Va.: Gano Books, 1982 edition of original 1857 edition published by The Southern Baptist Publication Society), pages 86-87.

8

KNOWING AND EXPERIENCING GOD'S LOVE

Central Idea
We can trust God's love, because He loves us with a perfect and infinite love, which was demonstrated on Calvary. Because of our union with Christ, we are secure in that love.

Examining Trust
It seems that the more we come to believe in and accept the sovereignty of God over every event of our lives, the more we are tempted to question His love. We think, "If God is in control of this adversity and can do something about it, why doesn't He?"

There is no doubt that the most convincing evidence of God's love in all of Scripture is His giving His Son to die for our sins. The extent of God's love at Calvary is seen in both the infinite cost to Him of giving His one and only Son, and in the wretched and miserable condition of those He loved.

Any time we are tempted to doubt God's love for us we should go back to the Cross. We should reason somewhat in this fashion: If God loved me enough to give His Son to die for me when I was His enemy, surely He loves me enough to care for me now that I am His child. Having loved me to the ultimate extent at the Cross, He cannot possibly fail to love me in my times of adversity.

If we are to trust God in adversity, we must use our minds in those times to reason through the great truths of God's sovereignty, wisdom, and love as they are revealed to us in the Scriptures. We must not allow our emotions to hold sway over our minds. Rather, we must seek to let the truth of God rule our minds. Our emotions must become subservient to the truth. This does not mean we do not feel the pain of adversity and heartache. We feel it keenly. Nor does it mean we should seek to bury our emotional pain in a stoic-like attitude. We are meant to feel the pain of adversity, but we must resist allowing that pain to cause us to lapse into hard thoughts about God.

The infinite, measureless love of God is poured out upon us, not because of who we are or what we are, but because we are in Christ Jesus. It is very important that we grasp this crucial concept that God's love to us is *in Christ.* Just as God's love to His *Son* cannot change, so His love to *us* cannot change, because are in union with the One He loves. God's love to us can no more waver than His love to His Son can waver. God does not look within us for a reason to love us. He loves us because we are in Christ Jesus.

God's sovereignty is exercised primarily for His glory. But because you and I are *in* Christ Jesus, *His* glory and *our* good are linked together. Because we are united with Christ, whatever is for His glory is also for our good. And whatever is for our good is for His glory.

God cannot forsake us because we are His children, in blessed union with His Son. We cannot be cut off from His sight. But we can be cut off from the *assurance* of His love when we allow doubt and unbelief to gain a foothold in our hearts.

The Bible's assurance of the sovereignty and constancy of God's love does not mean that we should not expect adversity. We mistakenly look for tokens of God's love in happiness. We should instead look for them in His faithful and persistent work to conform us to Christ. God in His infinite wisdom and perfect love will never over-discipline us; He will never allow any adversity in our lives that is not ultimately for our good.

God disciplines us with reluctance, though He does it faithfully. He does not delight in our adversities, but He will not spare us that which we need to grow more and more into the likeness of His Son. It is our imperfect spiritual condition that makes discipline necessary.

God's love is unfailing; His grace is always sufficient. But there is even more good news. He is *with us* in our troubles.

God's unfailing love for us is an objective fact affirmed over and over in the Scriptures. It is true whether we believe it or not. Our doubts do not destroy God's love, nor does our faith create it. It originates in the very nature of God, who is love, and it flows to us through our union with His beloved Son.

But the experience of that love and the comfort it is intended to bring is dependent upon our believing the truth about God's love as it is revealed to us in the Scriptures. Doubts about God's love, allowed to harbor in our hearts, will surely deprive us of the comfort of His love.

We are just as dependent upon the Holy Spirit to enable us to trust in God's love as we are dependent upon Him to enable us to obey His commands. But just as we are responsible to obey in confidence that He is at work in us, so we are responsible to trust Him in that same attitude of dependence and confidence.

With God's help we, too, can come to the place, even in the midst of our adversities, where we will be able to say, "I trust in Your unfailing love." *(Taken from chapters 9 and 10 of* Trusting God.*)*

Developing Trust

1. What observations about God's love can you make from these verses?

Psalm 103:11

Isaiah 54:10

Zephaniah 3:17

Romans 8:38-39

2. a. How does God feel about punishing the wicked (Ezekiel 18:23,32; 33:11; 2 Peter 3:9)?

   b. Read Lamentations 3:32-33. How does God feel about the afflictions He allows us to suffer when we sin?

3. a. In what event do we see the supreme demonstration of God's love for us? Read 1 John 4:9-10.

   b. Restate Romans 5:6-8 in your own words.

4. a. What experiences in your life have tempted you to doubt God's love?

b. When you have doubted God's love, what has helped you regain your confidence in His love for you?

5. a. Based on Ephesians 1:3-6, how does being "in Christ" affect God's love for us?

b. How does John 15:1-8 describe our relationship with Jesus?

c. If the Father loves Jesus, then, what are the implications for us?

d. What does pruning have to do with love (John 15:2)?

6. Read Lamentations 3:17-24.

a. What feelings did Jeremiah express in verses 17-20?

b. How did he deal with those feelings (verses 21-24)?

c. How do you deal with your feelings of discouragement and defeat?

d. What could you learn from Jeremiah about handling these feelings?

7. a. What can we learn from Hebrews 12:5-11 about why God disciplines us?

b. When have you experienced God's discipline? Describe one instance.

c. What lessons did you learn?

d. Did you sense God's love in the process? Explain.

8. God gives us the grace we need each day. We don't have the grace today for the "what ifs" of tomorrow.

 a. Describe a time when it was especially important for you to focus on God's daily grace without looking ahead.

 b. What happened when you tried to look down the road to see how you would cope tomorrow?

9. Summarize what God promises in the following verses.

Psalm 32:10

Isaiah 41:10

Isaiah 43:2-3

10. Read Psalm 13.

a. Have you ever felt as David did when he wrote Psalm 13:1-2? If so, describe those feelings in your own words.

b. How did David end this psalm (verses 5-6)?

c. How do you think it is possible to get from the feelings of verses 1-2 to the decision in verses 5-6?

11. a. To what extent do you currently experience God's love?

b. What do you think is the major barrier keeping you from feeling God's love for you?

c. How can you start to remove that barrier?

Trust in Action
1. Use a concordance to find other verses about God's love for us. Copy them into your journal.

2. Choose one verse about God's love and memorize it. Use it when Satan tries to convince you that God doesn't really love you.

3. Write a letter to someone who needs to know about God's love for him or her.

4. Write a letter to Jesus thanking Him for His love.

9

TRUSTING GOD FOR WHO YOU ARE

Central Idea
God created us with all our abilities and disabilities for His glory. We must accept ourselves and trust God's wisdom in creating us the way we are.

Examining Trust
Many people struggle to accept themselves as they are. For them life is just a continuous adversity, not from outside circumstances but from who they are. Their greatest need in trusting God may be to "trust God for who I am." For those with this need, Psalm 139:13-16 has some very important and helpful things to say.

Psalm 139:13-16 teaches us that we are who we are because God Himself created us the way we are—not because of an impersonal biological process. David says to God, "You knit me together in my mother's womb." He pictures God as a master weaver at work in our mother's womb. David also says, "For you created my inmost being." The Hebrew word for "inmost being" is literally kidneys, a word used by the Jews to express the seat of longings and desires. *The New International Version Study Bible* says the word was used in Hebrew idiom for "the center of emotions and of moral sensitivity." David, then, is essentially saying, "You created my personality." And just as God was personally involved in the creation of David, so He was directly involved in creating you and me.

If I have difficulty accepting myself the way God made me, then I have a controversy with God. Obviously you and I need to change insofar as our sinful nature distorts that which God has made. Therefore, I do not say that we need to accept ourselves as we are, but as God made us in our basic physical, mental, and emotional makeup.

David praised God, not because he was handsome but because *God made him.* The eternal God who is infinite in His wisdom and perfect in His love personally made you and me. He gave you the body, the mental abilities, and the basic personality you have because that is the way He wanted you to be. And He wanted you to be just that way because He loves you and wants to glorify Himself through you.

Self-acceptance is basically trusting God for who I am, disabilities or physical flaws and all. Certainly we will sometimes struggle with who we are. Unlike specific incidents of adversity, our disabilities and infirmities are always with us. So we have to learn to trust God in this area continually.

Psalm 139:16 says, "All the days ordained for me were written in your book before one of them came to be." There are two possible meanings that may be given to this verse. The first is that the span of David's lifetime, i.e., the number of days he would live, was divinely ordained by God. But it is likely that David had in mind the other meaning in this passage: that all the experiences of his life, day by day, were written down in God's book before he was even born. This refers not simply to God's prior knowledge of what will occur in our lives, but to His plan for our lives.

Just as we must trust God for who we are, we must also trust Him for what we are—whether it be an engineer or a missionary, a homemaker or a nurse. The realization that God has planned our days for us should not lead us to a fatalistic acceptance of the status quo. If we have an opportunity to improve our situation in a way that will honor God, we should do so. There has to be in our lives a delicate balance between godly efforts to improve our situation and godly acceptance of those situations that cannot be changed by us.

We do have a responsibility to make wise decisions or to discover the will of God, whichever term we may prefer to use. But God's plan for us is not contingent upon our decisions. God's plan is not contingent at all. God's plan is sovereign. It includes our foolish decisions as well as our wise ones.

I am where I am today, not because I have always made wise decisions or correctly discovered the will of God at particular points along the way, but because God has faithfully led me and guided me along the path of His will for me.

God's guidance is almost always step-by-step; He does not show us our life's plan all at once. Sometimes our anxiousness to know the will of God comes from a desire to "peer over God's shoulder" to see what His plan is. What we need to do is learn to trust Him to guide us.

Of course, this does not mean that we put our minds into neutral and expect God to guide us in some mysterious way apart from hard and prayerful thinking on our part. It does mean, as Dr. James Packer has said, "God made us thinking beings, and he guides our minds as we think things out in his presence."[1] God guides our minds as we think. He does not look down from Heaven at our struggles to know His will and say, "I hope you make the right decision." Rather, in His time and in His way He will lead us in His path for us. *(Taken from chapter 11 of* Trusting God.*)*

Developing Trust

1. What truth is being taught in the following verses?

Job 10:8-11

Psalm 119:73

Psalm 139:13-14

2. a. Do you ever struggle with accepting the way God made you? Explain.

b. What is your attitude about your physical appearance?

c. What is your attitude about your personality and inner character?

d. Is your attitude pleasing to God? If it is not, how could you change your attitude?

3. a. What characteristics about yourself do you need to learn to accept?

b. What characteristics should you try to change?

c. To what extent is it all right to try to change your physical appearance?

4. In lesson 5, we looked at Exodus 4:11 and John 9:1-3. How can these verses help us to accept our imperfections?

5. How can 1 Corinthians 4:7 help us keep our good qualities in the proper perspective?

6. Restate in your own words the truths taught in these verses.

Job 14:5

Psalm 31:15

Psalm 139:16

Acts 17:26

7. How can Jeremiah 29:11 encourage you when life seems overwhelming?

8. a. What advice does Paul give to slaves in 1 Corinthians 7:21?

b. What general truth can we get from this verse?

9. a. According to Psalm 23:2-3, what does God do for us?

b. Describe a time when you felt God's guidance in your life.

✳c. List some of the ways God can guide us when we are making a difficult decision.

d. Reflect on the last major decision you made. What method did you use to seek God's guidance and to make the wisest decision?

10. Read Acts 16:6-10.

   a. What specific guidance did Paul and his companions receive?

   b. We are not told how the Spirit prevented them from entering Bithynia and the province of Asia, but we know that He did. From these events what do we learn about God's guidance?

   c. Does God regularly guide you in such an explicit way? Why do you suppose this is so?

11. a. Which of the daily activities that you are currently involved in do you feel God wants you to be doing?

b. Which, if any, current activities do you think God may not want you to be doing? What makes you think that?

12. If you are discontent with your present position, do you need to accept where you are with a thankful heart, or does God want you to pursue something new?

Trust in Action

1. Take some time, in addition to your regular devotions, to be alone with the Lord and thank Him for creating you just the way you are. If you are angry about the body, the mind, the skills, the inabilities, or the personality God has given you, confess your anger and ask God to give you gratitude even for the things you don't like.

2. Memorize Psalm 139:13-14.

3. Make a list of the abilities God has given you. Think about how you are presently serving the Lord. Are you using your gifts and abilities? Can you identify new ways to serve that will better suit your abilities?

4. In Psalm 139:16-18 David expressed his praise and thanksgiving for God's guidance. Write a prayer expressing your gratitude for the way God has guided you to this point in your life. Thank Him for specific events that helped change your life.

NOTE
1. James I. Packer, *Your Father Loves You* (Wheaton, Ill.: Harold Shaw Publishers, 1986), devotional reading for October 13.

10
GROWING THROUGH ADVERSITY

Central Idea
Adversity causes us to develop Christlike character. For the believer all pain has meaning; all adversity is profitable.

Examining Trust

One of the many fascinating events in nature is the emergence of the Cecropia moth from its cocoon—an event that occurs only with much struggle on the part of the moth to free itself. The story is frequently told of someone who watched a moth go through this struggle. In an effort to help—and not realizing the necessity of the struggle—the viewer snipped the shell of the cocoon. Soon the moth came out with its wings all crimped and shriveled. But as the person watched, the wings remained weak. The moth, which in a few moments would have stretched those wings to fly, was now doomed to crawling out its brief life in frustration of ever being the beautiful creature God created it to be.

What the person in the story did not realize was that the struggle to emerge from the cocoon was an essential part of developing the muscle system of the moth's body and pushing the body fluids out into the wings to expand them.

The adversities of life are much like the cocoon of the Cecropia moth. God uses them to develop the spiritual "muscle system" of our lives. We can be sure that the development of a beautiful Christlike character will not occur in our lives without adversity.

Fortunately God does not ask us how or when we want to grow. He is the Master Teacher, training His pupils when and how He deems best. He is, in the words of Jesus, the Gardener who prunes the branches of His vineyard. The healthy vine requires both nourishment and pruning. Through the Word of God we are nourished (Psalm 1:2-3), but through adversity we are pruned. Both the Hebrew and Greek languages express discipline and teaching by the same word. God intends that we grow through the discipline of adversity as well as through instruction from His Word.

There are several things we can do in order to learn from adversity and receive the beneficial effects that God intends. First, we can submit to it—not reluctantly as the defeated general submits to his conqueror, but voluntarily as the patient on the operating table submits to the skilled hand of the surgeon as he wields his knife.

Second, to profit most from adversity, we should bring the Word of God to bear upon the situation. Martin Luther reportedly said, "Were it not for tribulation I should not understand the Scriptures." We might say, then, that the Word of God and adversity have a synergistic effect as God uses both of them together to bring about growth in our lives that neither the Word nor adversity would accomplish by itself.

Third, in order to profit from our adversities we must remember them and the lessons we learned from them. God wants us to remember them, not just as trials or sorrows, but as His disciplines—His means of bringing about growth in our lives.

It is helpful to consider some of the specific ends God has in mind when He allows adversity in our lives.

1. Pruning—God uses adversity to loosen our grip on those things that are not true spiritual fruit. In adversity we begin to relinquish our desires and expectations—even

good ones—to the sovereign will of God.

2. Holiness—Adversity causes us to grow in holiness, because it reveals the corruption of our sinful nature. What we have mastered in good times may quickly fade in adversity, showing us the need to go deeper in our battle against the rebellion of our wills, the perversity of our affections, and the spiritual ignorance of our minds.

3. Dependence—God teaches us through adversity to rely on Him instead of ourselves. Apart from our union with Christ and a total reliance upon Him we can do nothing that glorifies God.

4. Perseverance—God wants us to learn to do more than simply bear up under adversity. Perseverance is the quality of character that enables one to pursue a goal in spite of obstacles and difficulties.

5. Service—Adversity equips us for more effective service. It is necessary to make us into people who are fit for the responsibilities that God wants to give us.

6. The fellowship of suffering—Through adversity we have the privilege of entering into a special fellowship with other believers who are also in the throes of adversity. Suffering unites our hearts together in Christ more than any other aspect of fellowship.

7. Relationship with God—Perhaps the most valuable way we profit from adversity is in the deepening of our relationship with God. You and I obviously do not seek out adversity just so we can develop a deeper relationship with God. Rather, God, through adversity, seeks us out. It is God who draws us more and more into a deeper relationship with Him. *(Taken from chapter 12 of* Trusting God.*)*

Developing Trust

1. a. Think about the fruit of the Spirit listed in Galatians 5:22-23. How does adversity encourage each of the following:

love

joy

peace

patience

kindness

goodness

faithfulness

gentleness

self-control

b. Which of these have grown in your own life through adversity?

c. Did the growth you experienced endure after the adversity passed? Explain.

2. a. Read Romans 5:3-5 and James 1:2-4. What should our attitude be in the midst of adversity, and why?

b. How did Jesus maintain this attitude (Hebrews 12:2)?

c. How can we cultivate this same attitude?

3. What does Philippians 1:6 say about our spiritual growth?

4. a. What happens when we resist God's working in our lives through adversity?

b. What warning is given to us in Job 36:21?

5. a. Have you been drawn to God's Word in times of adversity? Why or why not?

   b. What portions of Scripture have become especially important to you during trying times?

6. a. According to John 15:2 what is the purpose of God's pruning?

   b. Even in the Church, Christians sometimes seek things that are not true spiritual fruit, such as position, success, and reputation. What counterfeit fruit have you been tempted to seek?

7. What is the connection between adversity (or discipline) and holiness, as expressed in Hebrews 12:10?

8. Read 2 Corinthians 1:8-9 and 12:10. How does adversity teach us to depend on God?

9. a. Hebrews 10:36 and 12:1 speak of the need to persevere. What is the goal of our perseverance?

b. How can we learn to persevere? (See question 2.)

10. a. Why does suffering deepen the fellowship between believers?

b. Describe a time when you experienced deeper fellowship through suffering.

11. What does Psalm 34:18 say about how adversity affects our relationship with God?

12. Which of the seven results of suffering—pruning, holiness, dependence, perseverance, service, fellowship, relationship with God—which are discussed under "Examining Trust," have you personally experienced?

Trust in Action
1. Memorize James 1:2-4.

2. Contact someone you know who is suffering. Offer to get together to pray.

3. One of the best ways to remember what God has taught us through different experiences is to write down those lessons while they are fresh. If you haven't started a journal, begin now by recording the lessons God has been teaching you lately. Then, sit down once a month and record your recent discoveries in your walk with God. Over the years this will have a big impact on how well you remember what God has done in your life.

11

CHOOSING TO TRUST GOD

Central Idea
We must choose, by an act of our will, to trust God in major and minor difficulties. We can do this regardless of how we may feel, because we know that God is sovereign, wise, and loving.

Examining Trust
For many years in my own pilgrimage of seeking to come to a place of trusting God at all times—I am still far from the end of the journey—I was a prisoner to my feelings. I mistakenly thought I could not trust God unless I felt like trusting Him (which I almost never did in times of adversity). Now I am learning that trusting God is first of all a matter of the will, and is not dependent on my feelings. I choose to trust God and my feelings eventually follow.

Having said that trusting God is first of all a matter of the will, let me qualify that statement to say that, first of all, it is a matter of knowledge. We must know that God is sovereign, wise, and loving—in all the ways we have come to see what those terms mean in previous chapters. But having been exposed to the knowledge of the truth, we must then choose whether to believe the truth about God, which He has revealed to us, or whether to follow our feelings. If we are to trust God, we must choose to believe His truth. We must say, "I will trust You though I do not feel like doing so."

Trusting God is a matter of faith, and faith is the fruit of the Spirit (Galatians 5:22). Only the Holy Spirit can make His Word come alive in our hearts and create faith, but we can choose to look to Him to do that, or we can choose to be ruled by our feelings of anxiety or resentment or grief. We are responsible to trust Him in times of adversity, but we are dependent upon the Holy Spirit to enable us to do so.

The whole idea of trusting God is, of course, based upon the fact that God is absolutely trustworthy. We must also lay hold of some of the great promises of His constant care for us. One such promise we will do well to store up in our hearts is Hebrews 13:5: "Never will I leave you; never will I forsake you." Because God will never leave you nor forsake you, you are invited in the words of Peter to "cast all your anxiety on him because he cares for you" (1 Peter 5:7). He is not just there with you, He cares for you.

There are three pitfalls in trusting God that we must be careful to avoid. First, during times of temporal blessings and prosperity, we are prone to put our trust in those blessings, or even worse, in ourselves as the providers of those blessings. In adversity we tend to doubt God's fatherly care, but in prosperity we tend to forget it. If we are to trust God, we must acknowledge our dependence upon Him at all times, good times as well as bad times.

Another pitfall we need to watch for is the tendency to trust in God's instruments of provision rather than in God Himself. We must be careful to look beyond the means and human instrumentalities to the God who uses them.

The third pitfall is that we are prone to turn to God in trust in the greater crisis experiences of life while seeking to work through the minor difficulties ourselves. A disposition to trust in ourselves is part of our sinful nature. It sometimes takes a major crisis, or a least a moderate one, to turn us toward the Lord. A mark of Christian maturity is to continually trust the Lord in the minutiae of daily life. If we learn to trust God in the minor adversities, we will be better prepared to trust Him in the major ones. *(Taken from chapter 13 of* Trusting God.*)*

Developing Trust

1. Read Psalm 56:3-4 and 1 Samuel 21:10-15, which is the historical setting for the psalm.

a. What emotions was David experiencing at the time he wrote this psalm (1 Samuel 21:10-12)?

fear

b. How much trust in God did David show in 1 Samuel 21:13? Why do you think this?

He went to extreme means but acted entirely & trusted - God.

c When David chose to trust God, how did his feelings change (Psalm 56:3-4)?

Lost his fear

d. Tradition says that Psalm 34 was written shortly after Psalm 56, after the crisis was over. How do you explain the relationship between David's statements in Psalm 56:4 and Psalm 34:4?

- David was in fear but Trusted He Lord & God delivered him.

2. a. Have you had an experience in which you chose to trust God despite your emotions? If so, what happened to your emotions after you decided to trust God?

b. Why do you think emotions work that way?

3. a. Why is God worthy of your wholehearted trust?

b. Is it possible for us to be worthy of His trust? Explain.

4. a. What attitude did Job express in Job 23:8-10?

b. In times of distress we must be careful that our feelings do not mislead us. Do Job's feelings contradict the truth of Hebrews 13:5? Why or why not?

5. Read 1 Peter 5:7. Is learning to trust God and cast our anxieties on Him something we get better at? If so, how? If not, why not?

6. Sometimes when we are anxious, there are things we need to do. Sometimes there is nothing we can do. Make a list of the things you are anxious about at this time in your life. Which things do you need to act on, and which things do you need to leave in the hands of the Lord?

7. a. Do you tend to forget to trust God when things are going well? Explain.

b. In what ways do we need to trust God in good times?

8. a. What contrast is made in Proverbs 18:10-11?

b. Do you get your sense of security from your achievements and possessions or from the Lord? How do your actions reflect this?

9. a. What does God promise us in Psalm 50:15?

b. What do we need to do after God answers our call, according to this verse?

c. In what specific ways might you do this?

10. a. Are you more able to trust God now than when you began this study?

b. If so, what has helped you most?

c. What help do you still need?

11. How would you explain to an unbeliever why you choose to trust God?

Trust in Action
1. For the next week keep a record of your anxious thoughts. Decide which thoughts should prompt you to action and which ones you need to leave in God's hands.

2. Memorize Hebrews 13:5 and 1 Peter 5:6-7.

3. Read a biography of a godly Christian leader. Notice especially how this person's trust in God grew through his or her life. A brief list follows. Check with your pastor or church librarian for other suggestions.

Adomiran Judson, by Faith Cox Bailey
A Chance to Die, by Elisabeth Elliot (about Amy Carmichael)
Daws, by Betty Lee Skinner (about Dawson Trotman)
George Muller: Delighted in God! by Roger Steer
The Hiding Place, by Corrie ten Boom with John and Elizabeth
     Sherrill
Hudson Taylor's Spiritual Secret, by Dr. and Mrs. Howard Taylor
Shadow of the Almighty, by Elisabeth Elliot (about Jim Elliot)
The Tapestry, by Edith Schaeffer (about Francis and Edith
     Schaeffer)
William Carey, by Basil Miller

12

GIVING THANKS ALWAYS

Central Idea
When we face adversity, we can trust God. In fact, we *must* trust God. In addition, we should respond to adversity with thanksgiving, worship, humility, forgiveness, prayer, and a heart seeking only God's glory.

Examining Trust
Because God is sovereign, wise, and good, we *can* trust Him. If we are to honor Him in our times of adversity, we *must* trust Him. In our trusting God, there is more at stake than experiencing peace in the midst of difficulties or even deliverance from them. The honor of God should be our chief concern. Therefore, our primary response to the trustworthiness of God should be, "I will trust God." But there are some corollary responses to trusting God that are also important. They provide tangible evidence that we are in fact trusting God.

The first corollary response we will consider is thanksgiving. Paul said to "give thanks in all circumstances" (1 Thessalonians 5:18). We are to be thankful in bad times and good times, for adversities as well as for blessings. Thanksgiving is an admission of dependence. Through it we recognize that in the physical realm God "gives [us] life and breath and everything else" (Acts

17:25), and that in the spiritual realm, it is God who made us alive in Christ Jesus when we were dead in our transgressions and sins.

The basis for giving thanks in the difficult circumstances is the firm belief that God is at work in all things—all circumstances—for our good. It is the willingness to accept this truth from God's Word and rely upon it without having to know just how He is working for our good.

We can see a very close connection between the promise of Romans 8:28 and the command of 1 Thessalonians 5:18, when we understand the literal translation of the words *in all circumstances* is "in everything." In the Greek, as in the English language, the words and meanings are very, very close. We are to give thanks *in everything* because we know that *in all things* God is at work for our good.

Another response to the trustworthiness of God is to worship Him in times of adversity. Worship involves a two-directional view. Looking upward we see God in all His majesty, power, glory, and sovereignty as well as His mercy, goodness, and grace. Looking at ourselves we recognize our dependence upon God and our sinfulness before Him.

A third response to adversity is humility. "Humble yourselves, therefore, under God's mighty hand that he may lift you up in due time. Cast all your anxiety on him because he cares for you" (1 Peter 5:6-7). On the one hand we are to humble ourselves under God's mighty hand—an expression equivalent to submitting with a spirit of humility to God's sovereign dealings with us. And on the other hand, we are to cast our anxieties on Him, knowing that He cares for us. The anxieties, of course, arise out of the adversities that God's mighty hand brings into our lives. We are to accept the adversities but not the anxieties.

Our tendency is just opposite. We seek to escape from or resist the adversities but all the while cling to the anxieties that they produce. The way to cast our anxieties on the Lord is through humbling ourselves under His sovereignty and then trusting Him in His wisdom and love. Humility should be both a response to adversity and a fruit of it.

Adversity often comes to us through the actions of other people. Sometimes those hurtful actions are deliberately directed at us. At other times we may be the victim of another person's irresponsible actions that, though not deliberately aimed at us, nevertheless affect us seriously. Therefore, the fourth response to adversity we must consider is forgiveness.

I have found that two truths help me forgive others. First, I myself am a sinner, forgiven by the grace of God and the shed blood of His Son. I have hurt others, perhaps not so often deliberately but unconsciously through an uncaring spirit or selfish actions. Second, I seek to look beyond the person who is only the instrument to see God who has purposed this adversity for me.

A fifth response to adversity is to pray for deliverance. A spirit of humble acceptance toward God or forgiveness toward others does not mean we should not pray for deliverance from the adversities that come upon us. We should pray for deliverance, and we should learn to resist the attacks of Satan in the power of Jesus Christ. But we should always pray in an attitude of humble acceptance of that which is God's will.

Above all else, our response to adversity should be to seek God's glory. We see this attitude illustrated in the life of the Apostle Paul during his imprisonment in Rome. Not only was he imprisoned but there were men, supposedly fellow ministers of the gospel, who were actually trying to add to his troubles by their preaching (Philippians 1:14-17). Paul's response (verse 18) is essentially, "It really doesn't matter what happens to me or how I am affected by all of this. The important thing is what happens to the gospel."

We have seen that God is trustworthy. He is absolutely sovereign over every event in the universe, and He exercises that sovereignty in an infinitely wise and loving way for our good. To the foundation of a life lived in communion with God, we must add what we have learned about God in this book—about His sovereignty, wisdom, and love. We must lay hold of these great truths in the little trials as well as the major calamities of life. As we do this in dependence upon the enabling power of His Holy Spirit, we will be able more and more to say, "I can trust God." *(Taken from chapter 14 of* Trusting God.*)*

Developing Trust

1. a. Read Luke 17:11-19. What two human responses to a blessing are illustrated in this event?

b. According to Acts 17:24-25 and 1 Corinthians 4:7, why should we be thankful?

c. Do you have a thankful attitude toward God most of the time, not often enough, or rarely? Explain.

d. Write a prayer asking God to help you have a more grateful spirit.

2. a. What does Romans 8:28 say about God working in our lives?

b. How does Romans 8:28 help us fulfill 1 Thessalonians 5:18?

3. a. What was Job's reaction to the loss of his children and property? Read Job 1:13-21.

b. What is worship? (A Bible dictionary might be helpful.)

c. What specifically helps you to enter into a spirit of worship?

4. a. Read 2 Corinthians 12:7. Why was Paul given a "thorn in the flesh"?

b. Has God ever used an adversity in your life to counteract your pride? If so, describe the situation.

c. Why does God cherish humility in us (James 4:6)?

d. What are major sources of pride in your life?

e. How can you change the areas where you are proud into areas of humility?

5. a. How does humility help us deal with mistreatment from other people?

b. Do you have a hard time forgiving others? Explain.

6. a. What sort of attitude is pleasing to God when we pray for deliverance from some adversity?

b. Is there ever a point at which we need to stop praying for deliverance? If so, how do we know when we have reached that point? If not, why not?

7. Of the six responses discussed in "Examining Trust"—thanksgiving, worship, humility, forgiveness, prayer, and a heart seeking only God's glory—which one is the most difficult for you? Why is this so?

8. Look at Isaiah 42:8. How can your actions better show that glorifying God is your top priority?

9. What are the most important ideas you have gained from this study?

Trust in Action

1. Write a prayer to God, expressing the ways you hope to trust Him more fully.

2. If there is someone you need to forgive, or ask forgiveness from, make a point of doing it this week.

3. Memorize 1 Thessalonians 5:18.

4. Ask a friend to join you for a brief time of worship. You may want to include Scripture readings, prayer, singing, and silence. Discuss what helps each of you to break past the barriers in your heart to enter a time of true worship.

5. Watch your attitude for one week. How often are you in a negative, complaining state of mind, and how often do you have an attitude of thanksgiving? Keep a record in your journal. Share your results with a friend.

SMALL-GROUP MATERIALS FROM NAVPRESS

BIBLE STUDY SERIES

CRISISPOINTS FOR WOMEN
DESIGN FOR DISCIPLESHIP
GOD IN YOU
GOD'S DESIGN FOR THE FAMILY

LIFECHANGE
LIFESTYLE SMALL GROUP SERIES
QUESTIONS WOMEN ASK
STUDIES IN CHRISTIAN LIVING

TOPICAL BIBLE STUDIES

Adam, Out of Eden
Becoming a Woman of
   Excellence
The Blessing Study Guide
Caring Without Wearing
Celebrating Life
The Creator, My Confidant
Crystal Clear
Eve, Out of Eden

Growing in Christ
Growing Strong in God's Family
Homemaking
A Mother's Legacy
Surviving Life in the Fast Lane
To Run and Not Grow Tired
To Walk and Not Grow Weary
When the Squeeze Is On

BIBLE STUDIES WITH COMPANION BOOKS

Hiding from Love
Inside Out
The Practice of Godliness
The Pursuit of Holiness
Secret Passions of the Christian
   Woman

Transforming Grace
Trusting God
Your Work Matters to God

RESOURCES

Curriculum Resource Guide
How to Lead Small Groups
Jesus Cares for Women
The Small Group Leaders
   Training Course

Topical Memory System (KJV/NIV
   and NASB/NKJV)

VIDEO PACKAGES

Abortion
Edge TV
Hope Has Its Reasons
Inside Out

Living Proof
Parenting Adolescents
Your Home, A Lighthouse